THE RAFFI CHRISTMAS TREASURY

THE RAFFI

Fourteen Illustrated Songs
and Musical Arrangements

Crown Publishers, Inc., New York

CHRISTMAS TREASURY

Illustrated by Nadine Bernard Westcott

ACKNOWLEDGMENTS

"Frosty the Snowman": Words and music by Jack Rollins and Steve Nelson; copyright © 1950 Hill & Range Songs, Inc. Copyright renewed, controlled by Chappell & Co., Inc. (Intersong Music, Publisher). International copyright secured. All rights reserved. Used by permission. Unauthorized copying, arranging, adapting, recording or public performance is an infringement of copyright. Infringers are liable under the law.

"On Christmas Morning": Words and music by Chris Whiteley and Raffi; copyright © 1983 Homeland Publishing (CAPAC).

"Petit Papa Noël": Words and music by Henri Martinet and Raymond Vinci; copyright © 1952 Editions Max Esching. Used by permission of G. Schirmer, Inc., agent of Editions Max Esching, Paris, France, copyright proprietor. International copyright secured. All rights reserved.

"Every Little Wish": Words and music by Raffi; copyright © 1983 Homeland Publishing (CAPAC). Includes portion of "Ode to Joy" from Beethoven's Symphony #9.

"Rudolph the Red-Nosed Reindeer": Words and music by Johnny Marks; copyright © 1949, renewed 1977 by St. Nicholas Music Inc., New York, New York. Used by permission.

"Must Be Santa": Words and music by Hal Moore and Bill Fredricks; copyright © TRO-Hollis Music, Inc., New York, New York. International copyright secured. All rights reserved including Public Performance for Profit. Used by permission.

"Douglas Mountain": Words by Arnold Sundgaard, music by Alec Wilder; copyright © 1964, 1965 TRO-Hampshire House Publishing Corp., and Ludlow Music, Inc., New York, New York. International copyright secured. All rights reserved including Public Performance for Profit. Used by permission.

"Old Toy Trains": Words and music by Roger Miller; copyright © 1967 TREE Publishing Co., Inc., 8 Music Square West; Nashville, Tennessee 37203. This arrangement copyright © 1988 TREE Publishing Co., Inc. International copyright secured. All rights reserved. Used by permission.

"Christmas Time's a Coming": Words and music by Tex Logan; copyright © 1951 Bill Monroe Music, Inc. Copyright renewed, assigned to Unichappell Music, Inc. (Rightsong Music, Publisher). International copyright secured. All Rights Reserved. Unauthorized copying, arranging, adapting, recording or public performance is an infringement of copyright. Infringers are liable under the law.

"We Wish You a Merry Christmas": It was Lindsay Roth's idea to have fun with this song by using some new words written by Sandra Boynton. Thanks, Lindsay and Sandra!

Published by Crown Publishers, Inc., 225 Park Avenue South, New York, New York 10003 and represented in Canada by the Canadian MANDA Group
CROWN is a trademark of Crown Publishers, Inc.
Manufactured in Italy

Library of Congress Cataloging-in-Publication Data

Raffi.
    The Raffi Christmas treasury.
    For voice and piano.
    Traditional songs and original compositions written by Raffi.
    Summary: Presents an illustrated collection of well-known Christmas songs as well as original songs of the holiday season written and sung by Raffi.
    1. Christmas music. 2. Songs with piano. [1. Christmas music. 2. Songs] I. Westcott, Nadine Bernard, ill. II. Title.
M1679.18.R23R2   1988   88-750620-

ISBN: 0-517-56806-3

10 9 8 7 6 5 4 3

CONTENTS

PART ONE
THE
ILLUSTRATED
SONGS

FROSTY THE SNOWMAN

Frosty the snowman was a jolly, happy soul,
With a corncob pipe and a button nose
And two eyes made out of coal.

Frosty the snowman is a fairy tale they say,
He was made of snow but the children know
How he came to life one day.

There must have been some magic
In that old silk hat they found,
For when they placed it on his head
He began to dance around.

O, Frosty the snowman was alive as he could be,
And the children say he could laugh and play
Just the same as you and me.

10

Frosty the snowman knew the sun was hot that day,
So he said, "Let's run and we'll have some fun
Now before I melt away."

11

Down to the village, with a broomstick in his hand
Running here and there all around the square sayin',
"Catch me if you can."
He led them down the streets of town
Right to the traffic cop,

And he only paused a moment when
He heard him holler "Stop!"
For Frosty the snowman had to hurry on his way.
But he waved good-bye sayin', "Don't you cry,
I'll be back again some day."

Thumpety thump thump, thumpety thump thump,
Look at Frosty go.
Thumpety thump thump, thumpety thump thump,
Over the hills of snow.

13

UP ON THE HOUSE-TOP

Up on the house-top reindeer pause,
Out jumps good old Santa Claus;
Down through the chimney with lots of toys,
All for the little ones, Christmas joys.

14

Ho, ho, ho! who wouldn't go!
Ho, ho, ho! who wouldn't go!
Up on the house-top, click, click, click,
Down through the chimney with good Saint Nick.

ON CHRISTMAS MORNING

Waiting
Throughout the year
For Christmas morning
To be here.
Counting
How many days
Till Christmas morning
Drawing near.

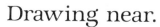

On Christmas morning
I'll wake up bright and early
Be the first one out of bed
With the mistletoe 'bove my head.
On Christmas morning
We can sing and celebrate
And make the feeling stay
All through the day.

16

Presents
Under the tree
There's one from me to you
And you to me.
Family
And friends are here
On the very best morning
Of the year.

17

PETIT PAPA NOËL
("Little Father Christmas")

In France, Santa Claus is known as Papa Noël or "Father Christmas." French children, instead of hanging stockings on Christmas Eve, leave out one of their shoes for Papa Noël to fill with candy and gifts.

C'est la belle nuit de Noël
La neige étant son manteau blanc
Et les yeux levés vers le ciel
A genoux les petits enfants
Avant de fermer les paupières
Font une dernière prière

It's Christmas Eve,
and snow is covering the ground.
As the children get ready for bed,
they each have one last prayer:

18

Petit Papa Noël
Quand tu descendras du ciel
Avec des jouets par milliers
N'oublie pas mon petit soulier
Mais avant de partir
Il faudra bien te couvrir
Dehors tu vas avoir si froid
C'est un peu à cause de moi

Petit Papa Noël,
with all those toys you are bringing,
please don't forget to fill *my* shoe.
But I don't want you to get cold:
I hope you bundle up before you leave.

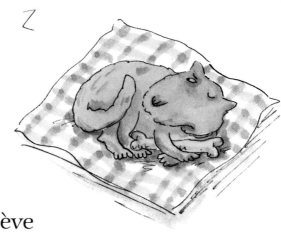

Il me tarde tant que le jour se lève
Pour voir si tu m'as apporté
Tous le beaux joujoux
Que je vois en rêve
Et que je t'ai commandé
Petit Papa Noël
Quand tu descendras du ciel
Avec des jouets par milliers
N'oublie pas mon petit soulier

I can hardly wait until morning!
I wonder if you will bring me
all the toys I've dreamed about—
I asked you to, remember?

Le marchand de sable est passé
Les enfants vont faire dodo
Et tu vas pouvoir commencer
Avec ta hotte sur le dos
Au son des cloches des églises
Ta distribution de surprises

Petit Papa Noël
Quand tu descendras du ciel
Avec des jouets par milliers
N'oublie pas mon petit soulier

The sandman is making everybody sleepy now....
It's almost time for you to start your trip.
But petit Papa Noël,
with all those toys you're bringing,
please don't forget to fill *my* shoe.

JINGLE BELLS

Jingle bells, jingle bells,
Jingle all the way!
Oh what fun it is to ride
In a one-horse open sleigh!
Jingle bells, jingle bells,
Jingle all the way!
Oh what fun it is to ride
In a one-horse open sleigh!

Dashing through the snow,
In a one-horse open sleigh,
O'er the fields we go,
Laughing all the way.

23

Bells on bobtails ring,
Making spirits bright,
What fun it is to ride
And sing a sleighing song tonight!

THE FIRST NOËL

The first Noël the angels did say,
Was to certain poor shepherds in fields as they lay;
In fields where they lay keeping their sheep
On a cold winter's night that was so deep.

Noël, Noël, Noël, Noël,
Born is the King of Israel.

They looked up and saw a star
Shining in the East, beyond them far;
And to the earth it gave great light,
And so it continued both day and night.

Noël, Noël, Noël, Noël,
Born is the King of Israel.

DECK THE HALLS

Deck the halls with boughs of holly,
Fa la la la la la la la la!
'Tis the season to be jolly,
Fa la la la la la la la la!
Don we now our gay apparel,
Fa la la la la la la la la!
Troll the ancient yule-tide carol,
Fa la la la la la la la la!

FOR
SANTA

FOR
REINDEER

See the blazing yule before us,
Fa la la la la la la la la!
Strike the harp and join the chorus,
Fa la la la la la la la la!
Follow me in merry measure,
Fa la la la la la la la la!
While I tell of yule-tide treasure,
Fa la la la la la la la la!

EVERY LITTLE WISH

Every little wish and every little dream
Has a chance of coming true at Christmas.
Every little song
Sung throughout the year
Has a chance of being heard at Christmas.

28

Every little prayer and every little hope
Is the joy of Christmas time.
All our loving hearts, beating all as one
Everybody fed, there's enough to go around
All our loving hearts beating all as one
The joy of Christmas time.

29

RUDOLPH THE
RED-NOSED REINDEER

Rudolph, the red-nosed reindeer,
Had a very shiny nose,
And if you ever saw it,
You would even say it glows.
All of the other reindeer
Used to laugh and call him names;
They never let poor Rudolph
Join in any reindeer games.
Then one foggy Christmas Eve,
Santa came to say:
"Rudolph, with your nose so bright,
Won't you guide my sleigh tonight?"
Then how the reindeer loved him
As they shouted out with glee:
"Rudolph, the red-nosed reindeer,
You'll go down in history."

MUST BE SANTA

Who's got a beard that's long and white?
Santa's got a beard that's long and white.
Who comes around on a special night?
Santa comes around on a special night.
Special night, beard that's white—
Must be Santa, must be Santa,
Must be Santa, Santa Claus.

31

Who's got boots and a suit of red?
Santa's got boots and a suit of red.
Who wears a long cap on his head?
Santa wears a long cap on his head.
Cap on head, suit that's red,
Special night, beard that's white—
Must be Santa, must be Santa
Must be Santa, Santa Claus.

Who's got a great big cherry nose?
Santa's got a great big cherry nose.
Who laughs this way, "Ho, Ho, Ho"?
Santa laughs this way, "Ho, Ho, Ho."
Ho, Ho, Ho, cherry nose,
Cap on head, suit that's red,
Special night, beard that's white—
Must be Santa, must be Santa
Must be Santa, Santa Claus.

Who very soon will come our way?
Santa very soon will come our way.
Eight little reindeer pull his sleigh,
Santa's little reindeer pull his sleigh.
Reindeer sleigh, come our way,

Ho, Ho, Ho, cherry nose,
Cap on head, suit that's red,
Special night, beard that's white—
Must be Santa, must be Santa
Must be Santa, Santa Claus.

DOUGLAS MOUNTAIN

Snows are a-fallin' on Douglas Mountain,
Snows are a-fallin' so deep,
Snows are a-fallin' on Douglas Mountain,
Puttin' the bears to sleep,
Puttin' the bears to sleep.

36

Trimmin' the wicks on Douglas Mountain,
Shinin' my chimney so bright,
Trimmin' the wicks on Douglas Mountain,
So God can bring the night,
So God can bring the night.

OLD TOY TRAINS

Old toy trains, little toy tracks,
Little toy drums coming from a sack
Carried by a man dressed in white and red,
Little one don't you think it's time you were in bed?

38

Close your eyes, listen to the skies.
All is calm, all is well, soon you'll hear
Kris Kringle and the jingle bells bringing

Old toy trains, little toy tracks,
Little toy drums coming from a sack
Carried by a man dressed in white and red,
Little one don't you think it's time you were in bed?

CHRISTMAS TIME'S A COMING

Christmas time's a comin'
Christmas time's a comin'
Christmas time's a comin'
And I know I'm goin' home.

Snowflakes fallin',
My old home's callin',
Tall pines hummin',
Christmas time's a comin'.

40

Can't you hear them bells ringin'
Bringin' joy to all, hear them singin'.
When it's snowin' I'll be goin'
Back to my country home.

Holly's in the window,
Home's where the wind blows.
Can't walk runnin',
Christmas time's a comin'.

Can't you hear them bells ringin'
Bringin' joy to all, hear them singin'.
When it's snowin' I'll be goin'
Back to my country home.

THERE WAS A LITTLE BABY

There was a little baby, oh my Lord
There was a little baby, oh my Lord
There was a little baby, oh my Lord
Way down in Bethlehem
Way down in Bethlehem.

They named the baby Jesus, oh my Lord
They named the baby Jesus, oh my Lord
They named the baby Jesus, oh my Lord
Way down in Bethlehem
Way down in Bethlehem.

They laid him in a manger, oh my Lord
They laid him in a manger, oh my Lord
They laid him in a manger, oh my Lord
Way down in Bethlehem
Way down in Bethlehem.

WE WISH YOU A MERRY CHRISTMAS

We wish you a Merry Christmas
We wish you a Merry Christmas
We wish you a Merry Christmas
And a Happy New Year.
Good tidings to you, wherever you are,
Good tidings for Christmas and a Happy New Year.

Good tidings we bring to you of good cheer,
Good tidings for Christmas and a Happy New Year.

We fish you a hairy Chris moose
We fish you a hairy Chris moose
We fish you a hairy Chris moose
And a Hippo New Year.

Good tidings to you, wherever you are,
Good tidings for Christmas and a Happy New Year.

PART TWO
THE
MUSIC

FROSTY THE SNOWMAN

Words and music by
Jack Rollins and
Steve Nelson

With a bounce

1. Fros - ty the snow - man was a jol - ly, hap - py soul, With a

corn - cob pipe and a but - ton nose And two eyes made out of

coal. Fros - ty the snow - man is a fair - y tale they

51

2. Frosty the snowman knew the sun was hot that day
So he said, "Let's run and we'll have some fun
Now before I melt away."
Down to the village, with a broomstick in his hand
Running here and there all around the square sayin'
"Catch me if you can."
He led them down the streets of town

Right to the traffic cop.
And he only paused a moment when
He heard him holler "Stop!"
For Frosty the snowman had to hurry on his way
But he waved goodbye sayin' "Don't you cry,
I'll be back again some day."

UP ON THE HOUSE-TOP

Brightly

Traditional

Up on the house - top rein - deer pause,

Out jumps good old San - ta Claus; Down through the chim - ney with lots of toys,

All for the lit - tle ones, Christ - mas joys. Ho, ho ho!

Refrain

53

Who would-n't go! Ho, ho, ho! Who would-n't go!

Up on the house-top, click, click, click, Down through the chim-ney with

1. good Saint Nick.

2. good Saint Nick.

ON CHRISTMAS MORNING

Words and music
by Chris **Whiteley**
and Raffi

Eagerly

Em A7 D D G

1. Wait - ing   Through - out   the

D Em D A7 D

year   For Christ - mas   morn - ing   To be   here.

D G D Em D A7

Count - ing   How ma - ny   days   Till Christ - mas   morn - ing   Draw - ing

D Refrain G A7

near.   On   Christ - mas   morn - ing   I'll wake up   bright and

2. Presents
   Under the tree
   There's one from me to you
   And you to me.
   Family
   And friends are here
   On the very best morning
   Of the year.

56

PETIT PAPA NOËL

Words and music by Henri Martinet
and Raymond Vinci

Freely

1. C'est la bel - le nuit de No - ël   La neige é - tant son man - teau blanc

Et les yeux le - vés vers le ci - el   À ge - noux

les pe - tits en - fants   A - vant de fer - mer les pau -

pièr - es   Font une der - ni - ère pri - ère   Pe -

tit Pa - pa No - ël Quand tu des - cen - dras du ciel A -

vec des jou-ets par mil - liers N'ou - blie pas mon pe -tit sou - lier Mais

a - vant de par - tir Il fau - dra bien te cou - vrir De -

hors tu vas a - voir si froid C'est un peu à cau - se de moi

Il me tar-de tant que le jour se lè - ve Pour voir si tu m'as ap - por -

2. Le marchand de sable est passé
   Les enfants vont faire dodo
   Et tu vas pouvoir commencer
   Avec ta hotte sur le dos.
   Au son des cloches des églises
   Ta distribution de surprises.

59

JINGLE BELLS

Brightly   Traditional

Jin - gle bells,

jin - gle bells, Jin - gle all the way! Oh what fun it is to ride In a

one - horse o - pen sleigh! Oh jin - gle bells, jin - gle bells, Jin - gle all the

way! Oh what fun it is to ride In a one - horse o - pen sleigh!

61

THE FIRST NOËL/ DECK THE HALLS

With feeling

Traditional

1. The first No - ël the an - gels did say Was to cer - tain poor shep - herds in fields as they lay; In fields where they lay keep - ing their sheep On a cold win - ter's night that was so

2. look - ed up and saw a star Shin - ing in the East, be - yond them far; And to where the earth it gave great light, And so it con - tin - ued both day and

63

EVERY LITTLE WISH

Words and music
by Raffi

Moderately

Ev - ery lit - tle wish and ev - ery lit - tle dream Has a chance of com - ing true at Christ - mas. Ev - ery lit - tle song Sung through - out the year Has a

66

RUDOLPH THE
RED-NOSED REINDEER

Words and music
by Johnny Marks

Merrily

Ru - dolph, the red - nosed rein - deer,

Had a ver - y shin - y nose, And if you ev - er saw it,

You would e - ven say it glows. All of the oth - er rein - deer

Used to laugh and call him names; They nev - er let poor Ru - dolph

68

69

MUST BE SANTA

Words and music by Hal Moore
and Bill Fredricks

Briskly

1. Who's got a beard that's long and white? San-ta's got a beard that's long and white. Who comes a-round on a spe-cial night? San-ta comes a-round on a spe-cial night. Spe-cial night,

No repeat—verse 1

2. Who's got boots and a suit of red?
   Santa's got boots and a suit of red.
   Who wears a long cap on his head?
   Santa wears a long cap on his head.
   Cap on head, suit that's red,
   Special night, beard that's white.
   Chorus...

3. Who's got a great big cherry nose?
   Santa's got a great big cherry nose.
   Who laughs this way, "Ho, ho, ho!"?
   Santa laughs this way, "Ho, ho, ho!"
   Ho, ho, ho, cherry nose,
   Cap on head, suit that's red,
   Special night, beard that's white.
   Chorus...

4. Who very soon will come our way?
   Santa very soon will come our way.
   Eight little reindeer pull his sleigh,
   Santa's little reindeer pull his sleigh.
   Reindeer sleigh, come our way,
   Ho, ho, ho, cherry nose,
   Cap on head, suit that's red,
   Special night, beard that's white.
   Chorus...

DOUGLAS MOUNTAIN

Words by Arnold Sundgaard
Music by Alec Wilder

Slowly

With pedal throughout

RH

D   Gmaj7   A7   D

1. Snows are a - fall - in' on   Doug - las Moun - tain,

Em   A7   D   Em   A7

Snows are a - fall - in' so deep,   Snows are a - fall - in' on

D   F♯   Bm   Em   A7

Doug - las Moun - tain,   Put - tin' all the bears to

72

OLD TOY TRAINS

With a lilt

Words and music by Roger Miller

Old toy trains, lit-tle toy tracks, Lit-tle toy drums com-ing from a sack Car-ried by a man dressed in white and red, Lit-tle one don't you think it's time you were in bed? Close your eyes, Lis-ten to the skies, All is calm, all is well, Soon you'll hear Kris Krin-gle and the jin-gle bells bring-ing. Old toy

74

If desired, the introduction may be played as an ending.

CHRISTMAS TIME'S
A COMING

Words and music by
Tex Logan

Brightly

Refrain

Christ - mas time's a - com - in'   Christ - mas time's a - com - in'

Christ - mas time's a - com - in' And I know I'm go - in' home.

1. Snow - flakes   fall - in',   My old home's   call - in',   Tall   pines

2. Holly's in the window,
   Home's where the wind blows,
   Can't walk runnin'
   Christmas time's a-comin'.
   Can't you hear them bells ringin'
   Bringin' joy to all, hear them singin'
   When it's snowin' I'll be goin'
   Back to my country home.

SILENT NIGHT/
AWAY IN THE MANGER

Gently

78

THERE WAS A LITTLE BABY

Sprightly   Traditional

1. There was a lit - tle ba - by,   oh my Lord,   There

was a lit - tle ba - by,   oh my Lord,   There

was a lit - tle ba - by,   oh my Lord,   Way

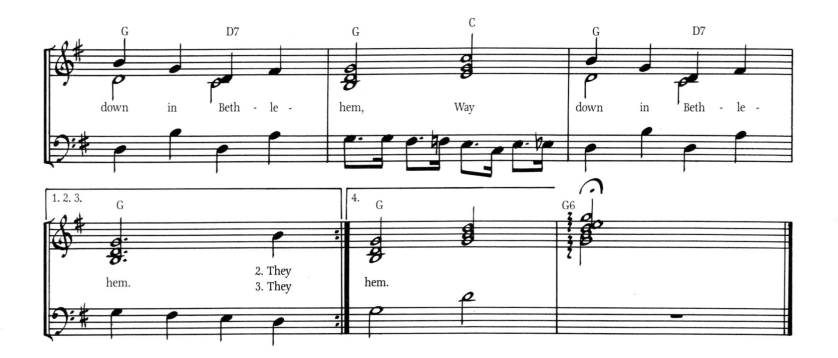

2. They laid him in a manger, oh my Lord.
   They laid him in a manger, oh my Lord.
   They laid him in a manger, oh my Lord,
   Way down in Bethlehem,
   Way down in Bethlehem.

3. They named the baby Jesus, oh my Lord.
   They named the baby Jesus, oh my Lord.
   They named the baby Jesus, oh my Lord,
   Way down in Bethlehem,
   Way down in Bethlehem.

4. (Repeat verse 1)

WE WISH YOU A MERRY CHRISTMAS

Spirited

Traditional

2. We wish you a Merry Christmas
   We wish you a Merry Christmas
   We wish you a Merry Christmas
   ...and a Happy New Year
   Good tidings we bring to you of good cheer
   Good tidings for Christmas and a Happy New Year.

3. We fish you a hairy Chris moose
   We fish you a hairy Chris moose
   We fish you a hairy Chris moose
   ...and a Hippo New Year
   Good tidings to you, wherever you are
   Good tidings for Christmas and a Happy New Year.

INDEX

The first number is the page on which the lyrics appear; the italic number is the page on which the music may be found. Away in a Manger/Silent Night *is an instrumental arrangement, so no lyrics are included.*